Highland Ra

Four Decades of Diesel Traction North of Perth

MIKE WEDGEWOOD

BRITAIN'S RAILWAYS SERIES, VOLUME 19

Front cover image: 37607 and 37218 head south at Slochd Viaduct on 6 April 2015 with Pathfinder Tours' 'Easter Highlander', the 08.18 Inverness to Eastleigh. This tour had visited Kyle of Lochalsh and Wick during the weekend.

Back cover image: In lovely evening light, 66110 pulls away from Kildonan at 18.55 with the 17.45 Georgemas Junction to Hartlepool empty pipe train on 17 July 2013.

Title page image: Shortly after leaving Kyle of Lochalsh, 37413 *Loch Eil Outward Bound* passes Badicaul with the Royal Scotsman touring train on 24 August 1991. The Cuillin Hills on the Isle of Skye can be seen in the distance. (Eddie Parker)

Contents page image: At Perth, an immaculate 37251 *The Northern Lights* and another class member lead a landcruise on 17 October 1993. In the early 1990s, InterCity ran a series of such trains, this one returning from the Kyle of Lochalsh and Far North lines. To the right of the landcruise, the maroon coaches and patrons were awaiting A2 60532 *Blue Peter* to couple up and return the excursion to Edinburgh. (Eddie Parker)

Published by Key Books
An imprint of Key Publishing Ltd
PO Box 100
Stamford
Lincs PE19 1XQ

www.keypublishing.com

ISBN 978 1 913870 94 2

Typeset by SJmagic DESIGN SERVICES, India.

All photographs are by the author unless credited otherwise.

Contents

Introduction..4

Chapter 1   The Highland Main Line 6

Chapter 2   Inverness and the Kyle of Lochalsh Line 36

Chapter 3   The Far North Line from Dingwall to Wick and Thurso 67

Bibliography..96

Introduction

My first visit to the Scottish Highlands was in 1977. At the tender age of 19, my interest in railways was developing and as a student studying geography who liked to travel, it seemed a good thing to do. On a sunny, warm June day I travelled by train to Fort William to see the glory of the mountains and lochs, and they did not disappoint. Mallaig was visited the next day when it was also hot and sunny. The next month I made a similar trip to Wick and completed the set with a third trip in September, this time to Kyle of Lochalsh. I was left with a lasting impression of wonderful railways, so different to those I knew at home in Doncaster, with distinctive motive power in the shape of Class 26s and 27s.

Sadly, those trips did not leave a lasting legacy of photographic images, as my camera of the time simply was not up to the job. So, when I got a Zenith E SLR in 1978, I was determined to visit again, which I did in 1979 and 1980 and it is images from those trips that are the earliest in this book. After one more visit in the 1980s, outings became more regular from the 1990s onwards, although unfortunately I have not been able to visit Scotland since the start of the Covid-19 pandemic.

My partner Janet could always be persuaded to take a trip to Scotland to coincide with a special train, so long as walking, birdwatching, history and good food were part the deal too. Inevitably, the number of these trips was limited as Inverness is not on our doorstep, being 420 miles and seven hours drive from home in North Lincolnshire! Through these visits, the attractions of the environs of the Perth to Inverness, Kyle and Thurso railways became more and more obvious to us. From a railway point of view, the combination of wonderful scenery, railway infrastructure and the wide range of motive power and trains on those lines suited my railway interests perfectly. Hence this book!

It is set out in three chapters, heading north from Perth where the magnificent station is the railway gateway to the Highlands. The first section covers the Highland Main line, which crosses the Grampian Mountains at the highest summit on British Rail at Drumochter to reach Inverness. The second chapter takes a look at Inverness before turning west at Dingwall to illustrate the scenic delights of the line to the west coast at Kyle of Lochalsh. The third returns to Dingwall to traverse the varied scenery of the Far North Line up the east coast to the most northerly point on British Rail at Thurso.

The pictures are arranged in journey order and the captions provide more details of the locomotives, places and scenery that are illustrated. I have tried to illustrate most of the different types of diesel locomotive and multiple units that worked regular passenger and freight services between 1979 and 2019, plus a selection of the special trains that have been operated over the years to enable visitors and railway enthusiasts to sample these magnificent railways. Set against the backdrop of wonderful scenery, impressive station architecture, infrastructure and Victorian signalling, this book offers a fascinating photographic journey through 40 years and over 350 miles of railway!

At this point, I must thank my friend Eddie Parker for the use of nearly 50 pictures from his extensive collection. His visits to the Highlands in the 1980s and 1990s fill the gaps in my coverage and contribute hugely to the contents of this book. He booked a holiday in Dingwall with his wife, Sian, the day before the Ness Bridge at Inverness collapsed in February 1989 and his excellent pictures that March record the Class 37s working winter timetable passenger trains. He also arranged a visit in March 1990 at very short notice upon hearing that there was thick snow in the Highlands and again these photos show the area as a completely different world. On other visits, sometimes travelling with his friend, Dave Myers, who sadly passed away early, he also did a splendid job chasing freights and weedkillers in the far north!

I also need to thank Dave Smith for filling another photographic gap, the use of steam heat Class 37s on service trains before the electric train heat fitted '37/4s' arrived, and my friend from school days Clive Olczyk for a couple of pictures from our 1980 trip. Thanks are also due to Tony Buckton for his excellent picture of the sleeper taken on his honeymoon in Dalwhinnie, his help with scanning some of the images in this book and his advice on technical issues in general. Particular thanks go to Janet, as without her enjoyment of Scottish holidays and tolerance of my hobby, this book would not have been possible, and I dedicate this book to her.

I could not complete this introduction without a mention of the Scottish weather. Its reputation is for rain and midges, but you will see very few wet day pictures in this book; I must be lucky, as I can only remember being rained off for one morning in Plockton, and even then it eased off enough to get the planned photo! There have been some days where interesting weather has produced interesting pictures with wonderfully clear light, and I hope you will understand my inclusion of more than one picture of the same train on some of these occasions. As for the midges, avoiding them is why there are lots of photos taken in spring! Finally, I hope that you the reader will enjoy this book as much as I have enjoyed putting it together.

In 2015, GB Railfreight became the traction provider for the new Caledonian Sleeper operation. Its solution for diesel traction to power the Aberdeen, Inverness and Fort William portions of the Highland Sleeper north of Edinburgh was to rebuild six Class 73 electro diesels dating from the 1960s with 1600hp power units. Previously only seen north of London on rare occasions, these interesting locomotives were available from 2016 and initially just worked the Aberdeen portion regularly, at first with a Class 66 as insurance. However, their introduction into service was problematic and they only took over regular operation of the Inverness portion in 2019, which I have no pictures of because of the pandemic! Therefore, for completeness, here is a picture of a Class 73/9 in Scotland working the 21.16 sleeper from Euston. 73966, the former 73005, is seen entering Stonehaven with the Aberdeen portion on the sunny morning of 13 April 2017.

Chapter 1
The Highland Main Line

The Highland Main Line from Perth to Inverness is a well-engineered route through rugged terrain. It begins at the impressive junction station at Perth, built in 1848, having seven platforms, two on the line to Dundee, three enabling access to the Highland Main Line and two for terminating trains from the south. From Perth, the line passes through Dunkeld, Pitlochry and Blair Atholl before climbing at gradients of up to 1 in 70 to the first of two summits at the Drumochter pass, 1,484 feet above sea level. Here, the line descends again through mountain country, with stations at Dalwhinnie, Newtonmore and Kingussie before arriving at Aviemore, centre for winter and summer visitors. Now climbing again, the next station is Carrbridge before reaching the second summit at Slochd (1,315ft). From here, it is downhill all the way to Inverness, sometimes at 1 in 60, using several impressive viaducts such as Findhorn and Culloden.

The line has a Highland Railway legacy in the architecture of its stations, along with the signal boxes and semaphore signalling that remains. It was opened as a through route in 1863 but initially running from Inverness to Aviemore via Nairn and Forres, giving a route mileage to Perth of 144 miles. In the 1880s, the current route was built via Slochd, reducing the mileage to 117. Much of the line is single track with passing places, though there is a long stretch of double track from Blair Atholl to Dalwhinnie. Signalling is still semaphore at Kingussie and locations south of there, except for Pitlochry, which was resignalled recently. Scottish government plans are to resignal and electrify throughout to increase capacity and reduce journey times and carbon emissions.

In 1979, there were ten locomotive-hauled passenger trains between Perth and Inverness each weekday, of which three carried sleeping accommodation. Class 26s were used initially in pairs from 1960, supplemented by Class 40s until '47s' took over. Today (pre-pandemic), there are 13 trains worked by Class 158 and 170 DMUs along with ScotRail's Inter7City short HST sets. This figure also includes one sleeper while the HST from King's Cross has been replaced by an Azuma.

Freight in 1979 was still a 'traditional' operation with wagonload freight in evidence and in 1988 there were two freight trains along the Highland Main Line, one each to and from Mossend and Millerhill. As wagonload traffic nationally contracted in the 1990s, Inverness was served via Aberdeen, this leaving the Highland Main Line with little regular freight. This changed in 1999, as Safeway started a daily container train from Mossend to supply its supermarkets around Inverness, although this train ceased in 2005 when Safeway was taken over and supply arrangements changed. It was replaced by a similar daily train operated by Stobart Rail on behalf of Tesco in 2008, which still runs today.

Another short-lived innovation was an express parcels train that ran from Walsall to Inverness. Cement has long been delivered by rail to Inverness from Oxwellmains near Dunbar, using wagonload services but, more recently, block trains have operated, initially by Freightliner on a weekly basis and then by Colas Rail today. There is also occasional freight destined for the Far North Line.

Over the 40 years from 1979, the line has seen a good variety of motive power working passenger, freight, and charter trains. This has ranged from Class 26s and 40s in the early days to long-standing favourites such as Class 37s and 47s plus the HSTs, '60s', '66s', '67s', '68s' and '70s' of today.

Arriving at Perth, 43114 *National Garden Festival Gateshead 1990* leads the 12.00 King's Cross to Inverness 'Highland Chieftain' on 4 August 1995. Perth power signal box can be seen on the right of the picture.

107746 in Strathclyde PTE livery waits at Perth to depart with the 07.58 to Edinburgh on 9 May 1990. It is standing on the east side of the station at platform 1, on the lines used by trains to and from Dundee and Aberdeen. First generation multiple units such as this did not see regular use on the lines north of Perth. (Eddie Parker)

47778 *Irresistible* is seen departing from platform 4 at Perth with the 15.40 Edinburgh to Inverness on 4 August 1995. This was the last year that locomotive-hauled trains were used to provide extra summer capacity, with one trip running each way between Inverness and Edinburgh from 2 July to 2 September. Waterman Railways coaches were hired together with a Rail Express Systems (RES) Class 47, as ScotRail no longer had such resources available. This '47' was previously 47081 *Odin*.

On 12 October 1998, 56034 *Castell Ogwr/Ogmore Castle* stands at Perth with an empty pipe train using converted BDA wagons with the addition of stanchions for smaller diameter pipes. At the time, EWS had contracts for pipes from Hartlepool to both Laurencekirk and Georgemas Junction for use by the North Sea oil industry, and for a short period Class 56s were regular visitors to Inverness with freight workings. A modern footbridge has since been built at this end of the station, which is out of character with this fine Victorian building. (Eddie Parker)

Stanley Junction is where the Highland Main Line diverged from the now closed railway to Aberdeen via Forfar, which ran straight on past the modern signal box, which dates from 1965. 66432's train shows the tight curve at the former junction as it passes with the 13.19 Inverness to Mossend intermodal carrying Tesco traffic on 8 May 2014.

At Dunkeld and Birnam, 33109 *Captain Bill Smith RNR* and 33116 *Hertfordshire Rail Tours* pass the splendid station with the returning 'Skirl of the Bagpipes' railtour from Inverness to Euston on 1 April 1995. This station was the last in Scotland to be lit by gas lights, these not being replaced until the early 1980s. Class 33s are very rare visitors to Scotland, although two were based at Aberdeen for freight work from 1999 to 2001 and those now owned by West Coast Railways have been occasional visitors in recent years. Both locomotives survive in preservation.

Class 50s occasionally worked the Highland Main line in the early 1970s, when allocated to the West Coast Main Line. Much rarer visitors since then, seen here are preserved 50031 *Hood* and 50049 *Defiance* passing Dunkeld with Pathfinder Tours' 'Orcadian' railtour, the 06.40 from Swindon to Inverness, on 16 June 2006. The locomotives carried the names and numbers of scrapped 50028 *Tiger* and 50012 *Benbow* on one side with the correct ones on the other, and the tour visited both Kyle of Lochalsh and Wick over the weekend. In the distance is Dunkeld signal box, built in 1919 and still operational today.

Just south of Pitlochry, the Highland Main passes under the A9. On 1 June 1990, 37707 passes this fine location with the Inverness to Millerhill Speedlink consisting of empty cement wagons. 37707 was the second Class 37 introduced into traffic in December 1960 as D6701 and was a regular on this service. Over a period of three years, the photographer saw this train four times and, on each occasion, 37707 was the rostered locomotive. It was finally scrapped in 2011 but only after it had received EWS livery. (Eddie Parker)

Seen from the footbridge, 26025 and 26031 arrive at Pitlochry double-heading the 10.35 Glasgow to Inverness on 28 August 1979. Class 26 locomotives were introduced in the Highlands to replace steam engines in 1960; they proved themselves to be reliable and continued in service into the 1990s. Double-heading of services such as this was common until the more powerful Class 47s became available. 26025 is preserved at the Strathspey Railway at Boat of Garten.

Pitlochry is one of two passing loops – the other is at Dunkeld – on the long 28-mile single-line section from Stanley Junction to Blair Atholl. Arriving at Pitlochry station on 28 May 1988 is the 6H25 Speedlink service from Millerhill to Inverness. While freight was not plentiful at the time, these wagonload workings could still be interesting and on this day included cement and some Ministry of Defence traffic. (Eddie Parker)

Pitlochry is a lovely Victorian town, known as 'The Gateway to the Highlands'. It has a beautiful Victorian station, built in 1863 at the same time as the line and is now Grade A-listed. Both the town and the railway were put on the map by the patronage of Queen Victoria. On 27 May 1988, the 06.55 Inverness to Glasgow Queen Street arrives at the station closely observed by the photographer's faithful border collie Brandy – a lover of railways, if only for the fact that a photographic expedition inevitably meant a good long walk! (Eddie Parker)

At 06.29 on 23 August 1993, 37071 and 37505 depart from Pitlochry with the 21.30 Euston to Inverness sleeper. Pairs of Class 37s were the usual motive power for this service from 1992 to 1995 and some were painted in InterCity livery specifically for this task, like 37505 seen here.

43116 leads the 07.50 Inverness to King's Cross 'Highland Chieftain' past the signal box at Pitlochry on 19 August 1993. In 2019, 28 years later, HSTs were still working this service, although Azumas have now taken over. The signal box, built in 1911, and semaphore signalling have now been made redundant as Pitlochry was resignalled in 2019.

68018 *Vigilant* passes the station at Pitlochry with the 13.19 Inverness to Mossend Tesco intermodal on 21 April 2016. This service runs six days a week and shows how the railway has adapted to modern commercial needs. The Class 68s work this service from time to time, but Class 66s are more regular performers.

Killiecrankie lies some three miles north of Pitlochry and on 27 May 1990, 47461 *Charles Rennie Mackintosh* heads south across the viaduct with an Inverness to Glasgow Queen Street train. The shot is taken from the spot known as the Soldier's Leap. In 1689, following a fierce battle in the Pass of Killiecrankie over discontent at the ousting of the Catholic King, James Donald Macbean, a member of the defeated government army was being pursued by Jacobite soldiers and his only means of escape was to jump 18 feet over a gorge above the raging River Garry. The photographer did not try it to see if there was a better shot on the other side! (Eddie Parker)

On 2 March 1990 there was still plenty of snow north of Blair Atholl but, nearer the town, the snow was rapidly melting with green fields beginning to appear. 47643 is seen approaching the town with the 11.42 Edinburgh to Inverness train. This locomotive is preserved by the Scottish Railway Preservation Society at the Bo'ness and Kinneil Railway. (Eddie Parker)

Crossing the castellated bridge over the River Tilt, 40185 heads south from Blair Atholl with a mixed freight on 27 June 1980. The signal box at the station can be seen in the background. Like the Class 26s, Class 40s were also amongst the first diesel locomotives to work over the Highland Main line.

A surprise development was the use of Class 67s on Highland freight trains. Built as express locomotives with working mail trains in mind, their use on lightweight intermodals such as this released Class 66s for other duties. On 18 April 2003, 67002 *Special Delivery* heads south at Blair Atholl with the 15.12 Inverness to Mossend Safeway intermodal. Built at the same time as the line, this station is a completely different design to Pitlochry.

37165 waits at Blair Atholl with the 09.45 (Saturdays-only) Inverness to Glasgow Queen Street for 158745 to clear the single-line section with the 09.55 from Glasgow Queen Street to Inverness on 21 August 1993. The signal box, built in 1890, and lattice post signal are fine survivors from earlier times. Locomotive-hauled trains such as this were operated for several years after the introduction of the Class 158 units to provide extra capacity in summer; however, they were only diagrammed for Class 37s in 1993 and 1994.

At Dalanroach on the 1 in 70 climb to the summit at Drumochter, 170411 passes as the 08.40 Edinburgh to Inverness on 25 June 2002. These units were built from 1999 onwards and were used on ScotRail from new. The disused signal box can be seen in the background, built in wartime to control an additional passing loop, which was replaced with double track running from Blair Atholl to Dalwhinnie in 1978.

Looking north from the same bridge as the previous picture, 66424 passes with the 09.23 Inverness to Coatbridge intermodal on 21 June 2010. This was a short-lived service as loadings were poor, as seen in this picture. Dalnacardoch Lodge can be seen in the background.

The history of Scottish sleepers goes back almost 150 years and, despite threats of withdrawal, they still run now with new rolling stock and rebuilt ex Southern Region Class 73 electro-diesels. The old order was in evidence on 28 May 1990, when with the heavily loaded 21.10 Euston to Inverness 'Royal Highlander', 47562 *Sir William Burrell* passes Dalnacardoch on the climb up to Drumochter. This locomotive is still in use as 47760 with West Coast Railways. (Eddie Parker)

Arriving at Dalwhinnie, on a trip to Scotland on 13 March 1989, the photographer noticed 26023 just setting off south working wrong line with an engineering train. Being told it was to drop stone at the side of the railway and as by then Class 26s were comparatively rare in Scotland, he set off back down the A9 to photograph it. The result is this fine picture taken near Dalnacardoch with the River Garry behind the train. (Eddie Parker)

Passing the closed station at Dalnaspidal are 158706 and 158738, forming the 11.52 Kyle of Lochalsh to Edinburgh on 24 June 2002. The train is leaving the Drumochter Pass where the summit of the line is situated. Dalnaspidal was the highest main line station in Britain at 1,405 feet above sea level before it closed in 1965.

Balsporran Cottages is a fine bed and breakfast establishment that I have stayed at for many years. Taken from the bedroom window is 66414 *James the Engine* in Stobart livery passing with the 05.14 Mossend Yard to Inverness intermodal run for Tesco on 26 April 2011. Drumochter Summit is in the pass behind the train.

67026 passes Balsporran, near Dalwhinnie, with the 05.40 Law Junction to Inverness parcels service on 22 June 2004. Operated for a commercial parcels firm, this service ran from 2002 to 2007 and was loaded only in the northbound direction with the coaches returning south empty.

Another picture at Balsporran, this is an evening view of 43314 leading the 12.00 King's Cross to Inverness, the 'Highland Chieftain', on 24 April 2011. 43314 was renumbered when it was re-engined from 43114, seen earlier in this book at Perth.

About two miles north of Balsporran and under a clear blue sky, 47747 *Res Publica* slows for its Dalwhinnie stop just after 07.00 on Monday 26 July 1999, with the 21.10 Euston to Inverness sleeper. (Tony Buckton)

Looking the other way from the same bridge south of Dalwhinnie, 37605 and 37259 make a fine sight as they pass with Pathfinder Tours' 'Easter Chieftain', the 08.17 Inverness to Cardiff (and Eastleigh) on 2 April 2018. I was very lucky to get this shot, travelling south from staying in Dingwall and, after photographing 37219 on a test train there, I arrived at this location just as the train was passing Dalwhinnie a few minutes late!

Sometimes the sun does not come out where you want it to! 37416 approaches Dalwhinnie station with the 13.38 Edinburgh to Boat of Garten 'Royal Scotsman' on 22 June 2004. EWS painted three Class 37s in maroon livery to match the Royal Scotsman stock, the first being 37428 then 37401, followed by this one.

In a busy scene at Dalwhinnie, 40062 arrives with the 16.42 Inverness to Edinburgh as 40197 waits to head north with the 15.25 Edinburgh to Inverness on 27 June 1980. Also in the picture are fire damaged 27202 and 25085, recessed with a northbound freight consisting of oil tanks and long welded rail. This was a somewhat lucky picture as the photographer and I were travelling on the Inverness bound train, got off to take this picture, and then nearly missed getting back on as the signalman was quick to set the road for it to leave! (Clive Olczyk)

37404 *Ben Cruachan* is seen arriving at Dalwhinnie with the 16.28 Inverness to Edinburgh service on 18 August 1993. From the look of the cloudbase, it seems I have been lucky with the light! This was one of the first Class 37/4s to be withdrawn, in February 1999, while other members of the sub-class are still operational in 2021. The signal box here dates from 1909.

In wonderful evening light, **37428** *David Lloyd George* passes the whisky distillery at Dalwhinnie with the 15.35 Edinburgh to Inverness 'Highland Enterprise' service at 18.25 on 18 August 1993. In the summer of 1993, two return trains from Inverness to Edinburgh each weekday and a third on Saturdays to Glasgow were booked to be hauled by Class 37 locomotives.

A different view looking in the opposite direction from the same bridge at Dalwhinnie as the previous picture was taken from. Power car 43044 leads the 08.00 Inverness to King's Cross 'Highland Chieftain' HST in snowy conditions on 1 March 1990. No doubt the passengers would have been happy with the comfort and warmth of their train, the photographer's recollection is that, with the air being quite still, he was not too cold either! 43044 has just been secured for preservation and repainted back into this InterCity Executive livery. (Eddie Parker)

Also on 1 March 1990, 47595 *Confederation of British Industry* passes the distillery at Dalwhinnie with the Inverness portion of the 22.15 service from Euston. This train also served Edinburgh and carried seated accommodation as well as sleeping cars. Surprisingly at this time, three out of the ten services between Perth and Inverness on a weekday conveyed sleeping cars, one being sleeping accommodation only. (Eddie Parker)

With the remnants of earlier snow on the ground, preserved 40145 *East Lancashire Railway* approaches Dalwhinnie with Pathfinder Tours' 'West Highlander', the six-coach 09.32 from Inverness to Braidhurst Down Loop running about 30 minutes late on 5 April 2010. This tour was an interesting one, half the train ran to and from Inverness and the other half to and from Fort William, with all passengers travelling all the railways involved via bus transfer across to the Isle of Skye via Kyle of Lochalsh and Mallaig. The two returning portions met at Braidhurst loop to return to Salisbury. It is worth noting that 40145 never carried this livery in British Rail service.

In much sunnier weather, 37259 and 37609 are seen heading south with another Pathfinder tour, the 08.17 Inverness to Eastleigh 'Spring Highlander', on 17 April 2017. This had visited Aberdeen and Kyle of Lochalsh over the weekend, 37605 was on the rear of the train having also been involved in the weekend's activities.

On 23 April 2019, one of ScotRail's 'Inter7City' HST sets heads north at Crubenmore, in Glen Truim, as the 08.33 Edinburgh to Inverness. Delays in receiving refurbished sets meant that unrefurbished HSTs were initially used, and various liveries could be seen on these trains. On this one, the rear power car 43144 is in de-branded First Great Western blue, the coaches in the same company's green livery and the leading power car in the correct ScotRail livery.

At Kingussie, 170393 and 158711 depart as the 10.52 Inverness to Edinburgh on 5 May 2006, running about 20 minutes late. The Class 170 unit is one originally built for use by Hull Trains. The fine station at Kingussie was built in 1893, after the opening of the line, and is one of the few still staffed in the Highlands.

Under threatening skies, 67019 departs with the 21.05 Euston to Inverness sleeper on 25 June 2002, running over an hour late at 08.15. At this time of day, it is notable that the sun is still on the front of the northbound train! Class 67 locomotives took over the operation of this train from Class 47s in 2001 and were replaced by rebuilt Class 73s in 2019.

66420 enters platform 2 at Kingussie with the 13.10 Inverness to Grangemouth intermodal on 10 April 2009. There is a good view here of the signal box, built in 1924, and starter signal, with Kingussie High School behind.

Aware that the days of internal loco-hauled trains in Scotland were numbered, and with a weather forecast of snow in the Highlands, the photographer set off for the Highlands on Wednesday 28 February 1990. A four days in seven Scottish Railrover meant that there was no need for a B&B as, at the time, in addition to the sleepers there were still overnight trains between Edinburgh, Glasgow and Inverness. There was also a lot of snow! Catching the first train out of Inverness on 1 March, on arrival at Kingussie, 37421 is seen preparing to give the 07.00 Inverness to Glasgow Queen Street assistance over the summit at Drumochter. This loco is still in service with Colas. (Eddie Parker)

Returning to Kingussie on 2 March 1990, 47604 *Women's Royal Voluntary Service* was photographed nearing the station with the 'Clansman', the 10.25 Inverness to Euston. Changing to electric traction at Mossend Yard, this was one of the longest trains to be seen on the West Coast Main Line. This service was introduced in 1974 but no longer runs, having finished in 1992. This was a result of the introduction of the 'Highland Chieftain' HST, which cut journey times to London by over three hours. (Eddie Parker)

Aviemore is visited here as 37240 calls with the 10.15 Inverness to Edinburgh on 20 August 1993. At this time, semaphore signalling was controlled from the signal box seen at the extreme right of the picture; however, modernisation has now taken place and the signal box is closed. The fine station was built in 1898, after the shorter route to Inverness had been opened. 37240 is still active on the main line, being owned by Boden Rail, finished in Transrail colours and occasionally used by Colas.

The Strathspey Railway now runs on part of the former main line to Inverness, which closed in 1965. The first station along the line is Boat of Garten, which is seen here between trains on 7 April 2010 with D5862 (31327) and D5394 (27050) stabled in the bay platform. Class 31s have never been common in the Highlands, although at the start of the dieselisation process one visited Inverness for trials in 1958. Also, one or two examples were used to power the 'Royal Scotsman' when West Coast Railways took over the contract in 2005.

The next station north of Aviemore is Carrbridge. On 19 April 2019, 43032 with 43163 at the rear pull into the loop to wait for the northbound sleeper to pass with the 07.03 Inverness to Perth empty stock. This was run for crew training purposes as, at this time, the HSTs branded as Inter7City were still being introduced into service. The front power car is wearing the new ScotRail livery.

This is an interesting train, the 11.35 Inverness to Mossend Enterprise, seen passing Carrbridge worked by 66106 and Royal claret-liveried 67005 *Queen's Messenger* on 8 June 2005. In the consist are oil tanks from Lairg on the Far North Line, container flats with a trial container for Tesco, and parcels vans at the rear. It combines two outward trains, the Enterprise, and the now empty parcel vans into one return working. Note that the signal at the exit to the loop is not illuminated, this only happens when a train is to use the loop, as in the previous picture.

Passing Carrbridge is Colas Rail's 70814 with the weekly 02.48 Oxwellmains to Inverness Yard cement. Despite being unstaffed, Carrbridge station is well kept and is still full of Highland Railway atmosphere, including the footbridge and waiting shelter. The station building dates from 1898.

47461 *Charles Rennie Mackintosh* is pictured at Slochd Viaduct running downhill from the summit with the southbound 'Clansman' from Inverness to London Euston on 15 September 1990. The climb to Slochd from Inverness is a challenging 23 miles with about 15 miles at 1 in 60 or 70. The 12-mile climb north from Aviemore is slightly less arduous, although the last five miles is mainly at 1 in 60 or 70. By way of comparison, the steepest gradient on the 31-mile climb from Carnforth to Shap Summit on the West Coast Main Line is six miles at 1 in 75. (Eddie Parker)

At Slochd Viaduct, Freightliner's 66614 passes with the 17.00 (Thursdays-only) Inverness to Oxwellmains empty cement train on 21 April 2011. Freightliner took over this working in 2002, when it became a lengthy weekly train; previously EWS had operated smaller loads daily as part of its Enterprise network.

The Lairg oil tanks are seen crossing Slochd Viaduct with DRS's 66434 heading south on 25 April 2011 as the 09.20 (Mondays-only) Inverness to Mossend. The Lairg oil tanks had several different operating arrangements in their 16 years of running from 2002 to 2018, at this time being worked north of Inverness by an EWS Class 67. The picture is made more interesting as the DRS Class 66 working an EWS train wears the Fastline Freight livery!

At Slochd Summit, the railway with its passing loop shares a gap between the hills with the A9. At 1,315 feet above sea level, both road and railway are susceptible to heavy snow and drifts. No such problems existed on 15 September 1990, as 47640 *University of Strathclyde* passes the summit with the 09.55 Glasgow Queen Street to Inverness alongside an unusually quiet A9. The railway also has passing loops at Tomatin and Moy before reaching double track at Culloden. This locomotive is now preserved at the Battlefield Line. (Eddie Parker)

Findhorn Viaduct was designed by John Fowler, who is perhaps better known as the designer of the Forth Rail Bridge. It is a quarter of a mile long and stands on granite piers that are about 45 yards high and traverses the valley carrying the River Findhorn. On 30 April 2020, it was lit up blue in support of key workers and NHS staff during the Covid pandemic. In happier times on 15 September 1990, 47635 *Jimmy Milne* crosses the viaduct with the 12.10 Edinburgh to Inverness. This locomotive is preserved at the Epping Ongar Railway. In the background is the A9 viaduct, which also crosses the valley here. (Eddie Parker)

On 10 April 2009, 67011 heads north on Findhorn Viaduct at 07.58 with the 21.15 Euston to Inverness sleeper service on its descent to its destination, which it will reach in about 30 minutes time. This is one of several impressive viaducts that make good photographic subjects on this part of the Highland Main Line. The picture is taken from the A9 bridge.

Climbing up from Culloden Viaduct, seen in the distance, is Colas-liveried 60076 *Dunbar* with the 17.59 Inverness to Oxwellmains cement empties on 21 April 2016. Colas had recently taken over this contract from Freightliner and its use of Class 60s was novel; this is the most northerly picture of one in my collection! When Colas sold its '60s' to GB Railfreight, Class 70s took over as seen earlier at Carrbridge.

Looking the other way from the same bridge on a minor road near Castletown, 37409 *Lord Hinton* and 37402 *Stephen Middlemore 23.12.1954-8.6.2013* descend towards Inverness with Pathfinder Tours' 'Easter Highlander', the 10.20 Aviemore to Kyle of Lochalsh, on 20 April 2019. The sight of two large logo Class 37/4s on this special train was most welcome, made possible by their use on Cumbrian Coast passenger trains finishing earlier in the year.

At Culloden, West Coast Railways' 37516 *Loch Laidon* and 37685 *Loch Arkaig* pull away from the impressive viaduct, with the 08.45 Kyle of Lochalsh to Carrbridge 'Royal Scotsman' on 9 May 2014. At this time, Class 37s were being used to Kyle rather than Class 47s because of a weak bridge. The viaduct has 29 spans and crosses the valley of the River Nairn, it is also the longest masonry viaduct in Scotland.

66102 emerges from the fog and passes the site of Culloden station with the 05.14 Mossend to Inverness intermodal on 22 April 2011. EWS took over working this train from DRS on 4 January 2010 but, on the first day of operation, the train headed by Stobart-liveried 66048 ran away downhill and derailed at Carrbridge station. Three days after this picture was taken, DRS resumed operation of this train on 25 April. Culloden marks the end of the double track section from Inverness.

With the city laid out behind the train, 47272 begins the climb out of Inverness to Culloden on Sunday 29 June 1980 with the 16.55 to Edinburgh. The array of semaphore signals can be seen, as well as the brick-built Millburn Junction signal box on the extreme left of the picture, which controls the junction of the line to Aberdeen. This locomotive became 47593 when fitted with ETH equipment and is still in use with Locomotive Services Ltd. (Clive Olczyk)

26023 passes the signal box and superb gantry at Welsh's Bridge with a carriage move, including the former LNER Manager's Saloon, on 13 July 1985. Sadly, the signal box and signals had gone two years later, but happily the saloon survives and until 2012 formed part of the prestigious Royal Scotsman train. The saloon with its viewing platform formed the social hub of the Scotsman, with comfortable armchairs and sofas and a well stocked bar, including some 30 malt whiskies varying from the strong malt produced by the distillery at Oban to the lighter whisky produced at Dalwhinnie. (Eddie Parker)

Chapter 2

Inverness and the Kyle of Lochalsh Line

The scenic attractions of the line to Kyle of Lochalsh are magnificent and well known. Service trains begin their journey at Inverness, which has a terminus station of seven platforms. The layout has a unique triangular arrangement, with platforms 1 to 4 curving southwards away from the concourse for Perth and Aberdeen services while platforms 5 to 7 curve northwards for services to Kyle and the Far North. A through line from Welsh's Bridge Junction to Rose Street Junction makes up the third side of the triangle and enables trains to bypass the station when travelling through the city between Perth or Aberdeen and the Kyle or Far North lines.

Inverness is the centre of many rail activities in the Highlands. Prior to 1987, Inverness had a fine array of semaphore signals and signal boxes, but today all this has been modernised and the Inverness signalling centre controls the Highland Main Line to Aviemore, the Aberdeen line to Elgin and all the railways north of the city. The latter use Radio Electronic Token Block (RETB) signalling, implemented between 1984 and 1988, where virtual 'tokens' give permission to proceed using in-cab equipment. Also ScotRail has servicing facilities in the city, which are evident to the visitor arriving at the station, being in the triangle of lines formed by the station.

Leaving the station for the north, the line crosses the River Ness on a new bridge, this replacing the old one swept away by floods in 1989. The line soon becomes single track and then crosses the Caledonian Canal at Clachnaharry on a swing bridge, operated by the only active signal box north of Inverness. The railway then follows the shores of the Beauly Firth, through reopened stations at Beauly, Muir of Ord and Conon Bridge, to arrive at Dingwall's fine station. Upon leaving here, the line turns west at Dingwall Junction, climbing to a summit at Ravens Rock (458ft) before descending to Garve.

A second summit is then reached at Corriemuillie (429ft), after which the line travels through Strath Bran to reach Achnasheen, just before the final summit at Luib (646ft). Gradients on the line can be as steep as 1 in 50 and it is a very winding route in places. The line then descends through Glen Carron to Strathcarron. From here, the line follows Loch Carron through beautiful west coast scenery to Stromeferry, the original terminus of the line when it was opened by the Highland Railway in 1870, the extension to Kyle being completed in 1897. After passing the attractive village of Plockton, views of Applecross, Raasay and the Isle of Skye precede arrival at Kyle of Lochalsh, 81 miles from Inverness. An outline map of the railways of the north of Scotland, including the Kyle line, is included in Chapter 3.

Trains on this line have never been frequent, three each way in 1979 and four today (pre-pandemic) with only occasional freight workings. Locomotive-hauled trains using first Class 26s and then Class 37s were replaced by Class 156 DMUs by 1990, although locomotive-hauled trains returned each summer to meet peak demand until 1994. Class 158 DMUs were introduced in 2000 and remain in use today. Charter trains operate regularly on the line, whether for enthusiasts, wine and dine landcruises or the Royal Scotsman touring train, which is a luxurious hotel on rails. Motive power on these charters can vary enormously, from Class 37s and Class 47s to Class 66s and more exotic visitors! Whatever the motive power, this is a superb railway and a great attraction for railway enthusiasts.

On the sunny morning of 31 March 1993, 37170 and 37251 *The Northern Lights* have arrived at 07.30 on platform 2 with InterCity's 'Cock of the North' landcruise, having left King's Cross at 19.25 the previous evening. These trips were effectively a hotel on wheels, with patrons both eating and sleeping on board. I travelled in a sleeping car on this train from York, but I do not remember getting much sleep!

47005 is seen departing Inverness from platform 3 with the 1T20 09.20 Inverness to Glasgow Queen Street on 7 August 1985. The photographer took this shot on travels around Scotland on a Freedom of Scotland Railrover. (Dave Smith)

On the wet morning of 30 June 1980, 27007 awaits departure from platform 1 with the 08.27 to Aberdeen. Steam heat is in evidence! Class 27s, more powerful than their Class 26 relations, were regularly used on these services but not the lines north of Inverness. This locomotive survives in preservation at the Caledonian Railway, Brechin.

For many years, trains from the Far North and Kyle lines used to run past the station at Inverness and then reverse into the southbound platforms from Welsh's Bridge Junction. This added a few minutes to journey times but meant the locomotive could quickly be released after arrival. Here, 26045 shunts past Loco Box after such a manoeuvre with the 11.15 from Wick on Sunday 29 June 1980.

After catching the night train from Carlisle, and wanting to photograph the mechanical signalling at Inverness, the photographer was surprised on arrival to find a Derby Lightweight DMU formed of DB975007 and DB975008 stabled there, the Ultrasonic Test Train. The date was 13 July 1985. This unit was converted in 1970 from cars numbered M79018 and M79612, respectively, and is now preserved at the Ecclesbourne Valley Railway. (Eddie Parker)

Inverness depot always had plenty of locomotives on shed at this time, usually Class 26s, 37s and 47s and permission to look round could often be obtained. No permission was needed for this photograph taken on 13 July 1985 though! It shows stabled Class 47s, Loco Box, two snowploughs and some of the semaphore signals in that area. (Eddie Parker)

37419 is seen arriving past Rose Street signal box with the 11.30 from Kyle of Lochalsh on 29 July 1986. At this time, all passenger services north of Inverness were normally in the hands of Class 37/4 locomotives, with eight allocated to Inverness, numbered 37414 to 37421. All of these eight were refurbished in 1985 specifically for use on long rural routes such as these. 37419 is still in service with DRS.

In an earlier view showing the old order, 26042 leaves Inverness with the 10.30 to Kyle of Lochalsh on 27 August 1979. Rose Street signal box is seen from a different angle and the signal in the foreground with shortened arms is of particular interest.

The date is now 18 August 1993 and Class 156 Super Sprinter units have taken over most daily passenger services. However, these did not provide sufficient accommodation for peak tourist trains, so Class 37s continued to work some trains. 37232 *The Institution of Railway Signal Engineers* departs from Inverness with one such working, the 10.25 for Kyle of Lochalsh.

47550 is seen arriving at Inverness with a freight train from the Far North Line on 27 August 1979. The wagons are Covhops, which will probably have originated from the aluminium smelter at Invergordon and were used to deliver alumina. The fine signal gantry indicates that it is taking the Rose Street curve to avoid the station. In the background, the track becomes single line just before the Ness Bridge, and on the right the docks branch is in use as a coal depot.

In 2001, the docks branch had a different use, the coal depot has closed, and the area is in use as a loading and unloading area for the Safeway container train. 37428 is waiting to shunt the wagons prior to their departure on the 13.30 Enterprise service to Mossend Yard on 15 October.

26007 and 26001 *Eastfield* pass Clachnaharry with the 12.35 Inverness to Kyle of Lochalsh on 18 August 1993. At this time, the Class 26s were coming to the end of their careers, their home depot of Eastfield in Glasgow was closing, and this pair was repainted in their original BR green livery to mark these events. Their duties included this working to Kyle each Wednesday in the summer. The signal box here controls the swing bridge and is the only one remaining open north of Inverness. In the background is the Kessock Bridge, which takes the A9 across the Moray Firth to the Black Isle, helping to significantly shorten the road journey. These locomotives are both preserved, at the Bodmin and Wenford and Caledonian railways, respectively.

Looking the other way from the footbridge at Clachnaharry, 37401, newly named *The Royal Scotsman* and painted in matching livery, heads south with the 13.25 Kyle of Lochalsh to Dundee 'Royal Scotsman' on 30 May 2001. The Beauly Firth can be seen in the background; on the left, the pub beer garden provides a pleasant place to spend a lunchtime in better weather! This popular locomotive is still in service with DRS.

At Muir of Ord, 158723 calls forming the 15.23 Aberdeen to Kyle of Lochalsh on 28 May 2001. This station was closed in 1960, along with all the others between Inverness and Dingwall, but it was reopened in 1976. Behind the train are the maltings, which used to generate significant freight traffic, and on the right of the railway is the shed, which was the maintenance depot for rolling stock marooned north of Inverness when the Ness Bridge collapsed in February 1989. Muir is the only passing loop between Dingwall and Inverness, which can cause delays on what is now a busy single line.

Beauly station reopened in 2002 and here 158714 is seen departing with the 13.46 Kyle of Lochalsh to Inverness on 3 April 2015. The short platform kept the cost of reopening down, but its length means that the guard can only open one door for passengers to exit or board. Nevertheless, the opening has been successful, the station had 46,510 passengers in 2019–20, the fourth highest on the line after Kyle of Lochalsh, Dingwall and Muir of Ord. Conon Bridge station also reopened in 2013 with a short platform and it too is well used. The old station building is behind the train.

On 1 June 1988, 37418 *An Comunn Gaidhealach* is seen arriving at Dingwall with the 10.15 Inverness to Kyle of Lochalsh. The origin of the RETB system that would then control 37418's journey to Kyle was born in January 1978 when atrocious weather hit the Far North. Seventy passengers were stranded north of Forsinard on a train in heavy snow drifts and were only rescued by helicopter 24 hours later. In addition, 40 miles of telegraph poles and wires were brought down. It was decided then that the simplest way of replacing the equipment was by use of radios, at the time maintaining contact between signal boxes but later under RETB control directly between trains and the signalling centre. Dingwall South signal box can be seen in the distance. (Eddie Parker)

Having read that RETB signalling had been introduced north of Inverness, when the photographer arrived at Dingwall on 31 May 1988 to photograph 37418 arriving on the 07.10 Kyle of Lochalsh to Inverness, he was delighted to find the semaphore signalling still operational. Mechanical signalling on the Kyle and Far North lines had been replaced in 1984 and 1985 with the RETB system controlled from Dingwall. However, it was later in 1988 that Dingwall succumbed to RETB with control moving to the Inverness signalling centre. Consideration had been given to extending conventional modern signalling from Inverness to Dingwall as part of the area's signalling modernisation, but this option was not taken up. 37418 is preserved but currently on hire to Colas for main line use. (Eddie Parker)

Dingwall has a passing loop and is the junction where the Kyle and Far North lines diverge. 37260 *Radio Highland* stands at the attractive station, built in 1862 when the line opened, with a ballast train for the Kyle line in May 1988. This locomotive and others with steam heating equipment worked the service trains in the early 1980s, having taken over from the Class 26s, until Class 37/4s with electric train heating equipment took over in the mid-1980s. (Eddie Parker)

On 31 May 1988, 37114 *Dunrobin Castle* arrives at Dingwall with the 7H37 freight service from Inverness to Lairg formed of oil tanks. This traffic ceased when the Ness Bridge collapsed in 1989 but was reintroduced in 2002. A government grant enabled this and other oil traffic from Grangemouth to return to rail, running until 2018. (Eddie Parker)

Passenger trains north of Inverness used to have a wider role than they do today. In particular, carrying mail, newspapers and parcels was important as can be seen in this picture at Dingwall. Three postal vans have met the 06.15 Inverness to Wick and Thurso hauled by 26031 on 28 June 1979, and similar scenes would take place at other stations along the route. Several parcels and brake vehicles are included in the train to deal with this traffic, which ceased when DMUs took over from locomotive-hauled trains as they did not have sufficient space available.

Over the weekend of 18 to 21 June 2010, Spitfire Railtours ran the 'Highlander', a special train from Crewe to Kyle of Lochalsh and the Far North Line. 37610 *T.S. (Ted) Cassidy 14.5.61-6.4.08* and 37608 are seen returning the train as the 16.10 from Kyle of Lochalsh on 19 June. Heading in the opposite direction are 158721 and 158709 as the 17.52 Inverness to Kyle of Lochalsh and Wick. This train would be split here, with 158721 (out of sight) running to Kyle and 158709 proceeding to Wick a few minutes later.

An elusive train on the Far North Line is the nuclear waste train to Sellafield, which arises from the decommissioning of the nuclear facility at Dounreay on the north coast. Here, 37602 and 37605 top and tail one nuclear flask and barrier wagons departing from Dingwall with the southbound 14.00 Georgemas Junction to Carlisle Kingmoor working at 19.05 on 9 May 2014. A journey of over 12 hours for these veteran locomotives travelling about half the length of the British Isles!

On the sunny morning of Sunday 1 April 2018, 37259 and 37605 arrive at Dingwall with Pathfinder Tours' 'Easter Chieftain', the 09.13 Inverness to Kyle of Lochalsh. This tour had originated at Eastleigh and visited Inverurie (for Aberdeen and local attractions) on the Saturday. Dingwall has a staffed ticket office and privately run café. Catering here was somewhat different in World War One when the railway played a key role, with military specials being run daily from Euston to Thurso for the Grand Fleet at Scapa Flow. A plaque on the station recalls that 134,864 cups of tea were served here to servicemen enduring this 22-hour journey!

The next morning, with frost on the hills and the temperature below zero, *37219 Jonty Jarvis 8-12-1998 to 18 3-2005* arrives at Dingwall with the 03.51 Georgemas Junction to Inverness test train at 08.55 on 2 April 2018. The bridge the train is passing under has replaced the lattice structure seen in the earlier 1979 picture and behind the locomotive and waiting rooms is Ross County FC's football ground.

At Dingwall Junction, 57001 is about to meet the line from the Far North with the 08.45 Kyle of Lochalsh to Carrbridge 'Royal Scotsman' on 19 June 2011. This locomotive was formerly 47356 and was converted in 1998 for Freightliner use by the replacement of its original power unit with a General Motors machine.

When the railway to Kyle of Lochalsh was built, it had to avoid Strathpeffer, the main settlement on its preferred route, because of opposition from a local landowner. The result was that the railway now has to climb to Raven's Rock summit to bypass the town. Here, 37218 and 37607 begin the climb at Fodderty with Pathfinder Tours' 'Easter Highlander', the 11.05 Inverness to Kyle of Lochalsh on 4 April 2015. This tour originated at Eastleigh and visited Thurso and Wick next day. A branch line was eventually built to Strathpeffer in 1885, which closed completely in 1951.

Garve is the first station and passing loop after Dingwall on the Kyle line, and here 26025 departs at 07.40 with the 07.05 Dingwall to Kyle of Lochalsh on 27 August 1979. This train ran empty from Inverness to Dingwall to provide a connection out of the preceding Inverness to Wick service. At this time, semaphore signalling was still in use. Highland Railway practice was to have two cabins at either end of a passing loop, with the token instruments in the main station building. Both cabins can be seen in this picture, together with evidence of freight activity in the yard on the right of the train.

The next train at Garve that day was 26041, arriving past the west cabin with the 07.00 Kyle of Lochalsh to Inverness at 08.47, as steam leaks from the heating pipe on the train. Much has changed since this picture was taken: the signal box and signals have been removed being replaced by radio signalling in 1984, the single track road bridge behind the train is now a level crossing, and the sidings on the left have been removed being replaced by an engineers' siding at the other end of the station. The station building remains today as a private house.

An unusual sight at Garve, as 20901 *Nancy* and 20904 *Janis* arrive with the Chipman weedkilling train from Kyle of Lochalsh on 31 July 1996. They are running coupled cab to cab, usually avoided with Class 20s as the forward view from the cab of the leading locomotive is restricted; certainly, the only time the photographer has seen such a combination! This train normally ran top and tailed but 20904, which was to lead the train, had failed so 20901 ran round to head the train back to Inverness. Class 20s were among the first types of diesel locomotive that replaced steam in the Highlands in the early 1960s. (Eddie Parker)

Seen from the war memorial, 37416 *Sir Robert McAlpine/Concrete Bob* and 37411 *The Scottish Railway Preservation Society* depart from Garve with the 06.05 Dunbar to Kyle of Lochalsh on 26 May 2001. This train was run by the Scottish Railway Preservation Society (SRPS), which operates a programme of tours most years using its own set of coaches. Loch Garve can be seen in the distance, the railway and A835 run along its southern shore.

Achanalt Viaduct crosses the River Bran where Loch a' Chuilinn to the east and Loch Achanalt meet. In this autumnal picture, 37417 and 37401 cross at 09.20 with UK Railtours' 'Autumn Highlander', the 07.20 Inverness to Kyle of Lochalsh landcruise on 18 October 2008. This tour originated at London King's Cross.

On 20 August 1991, InterCity-liveried 37409 *Loch Awe* makes a fine sight as it crosses Achanallt Viaduct with the 12.27 Inverness to Kyle of Lochalsh service. The photograph is taken from the aptly named Fisherman's Foot Crossing. A few miles to the east is Loch Luichart where in 1954, owing to the building of a hydro-electric scheme, the line had to be diverted for two miles and a new station built. This locomotive is still in service with DRS and appears elsewhere in this book in the company's corporate livery and in BR large logo blue. (Eddie Parker)

Achnasheen station is the next passing loop after Garve heading west. 26018 is stood in this picture, waiting for the morning train from Kyle to arrive before it can depart with the 07.05 Dingwall to Kyle of Lochalsh on 28 June 1980. Achnasheen's west signal cabin is seen at the east end of the station platform.

Later the same day, 26027 is seen arriving at Achnasheen with the 17.45 Inverness to Kyle of Lochalsh service at 19.19, as 26024 waits to depart with the 17.55 Kyle of Lochalsh to Inverness. The east signal cabin can be seen behind the approaching train, with a fine lattice post signal and the goods shed on the left. In the siding are wagons awaiting the next pick-up goods train while this siding still remains for engineering purposes.

On 16 March 1989, 37415 nears Achnasheen with a Dingwall to Kyle of Lochalsh service; the wide Strath Bran that the railway follows from Achanallt can be seen behind the train. This is just after the Ness Bridge collapsed on 8 February and, fortunately, sufficient locomotives and coaches were stranded north of the bridge to run a full service. Rail passengers used buses between Inverness and Dingwall. Later that year, Class 156s were moved across by low-loaders to work these trains. Fears were expressed that the bridge collapse might mean the end for the Far North and Kyle lines. With great credit, the bridge was rebuilt and on 9 May 1990, just 15 months later, the new bridge was opened. (Eddie Parker)

37407 Loch Long is seen waiting to depart from Achnasheen with the 12.27 Inverness to Kyle of Lochalsh service on 12 July 1991, running ten minutes late. To the left of the locomotive is the station building and to the right of that the Achnasheen Hotel, my accommodation for the night but which sadly burnt down several years later. At this time, the summer service was shared between Class 156 DMUs and Class 37-hauled trains to provide extra capacity, the green and cream coach livery providing some distinctiveness for these services. This locomotive is still in service with DRS.

Achnasheen is a small, scattered settlement and this is seen to good effect in this picture. While only a small village, when rail carried most freight and the mail it was an important distribution point for Wester Ross to Gairloch and beyond. Connecting buses also ran from here. Today, these locations are now served by road transport and the buses run direct. In this picture, 37416 has just departed from Achnasheen with the 10.46 Dingwall to Kyle of Lochalsh service on 1 June 1989. It has a dented nose arising from an altercation with a tree! (Eddie Parker)

On 1 June 1989, 37416 is seen approaching Achnasheen with the 17.00 Kyle of Lochalsh to Dingwall. It is travelling slowly downhill from Luib Summit past Loch Gowan, with some snow on the hills beyond. In summer, this train and the outward 10.46 from Dingwall included an observation car numbered 6300, which was converted from Class 101 DMU driving trailer 56356 and seen here behind the locomotive. A supplement was payable to travel in it, and a commentary on the journey was provided. (Eddie Parker)

In Glen Carron, 37610 *T.S. (Ted) Cassidy 14.5.61-6.4.08* and 37423 *Spirit of the Lakes* are seen climbing to Luib Summit with Pathfinder Tours' 'Cock of the North' landcruise, the 16.05 Kyle of Lochalsh to Inverness, on Saturday 9 October 2010. Near here, a private station was provided for Glencarron Lodge, but it closed in 1964. This tour also visited Thurso and Wick on the next day.

On 22 August 1991, 37428 *David Lloyd George* arrives at Strathcarron station with the 17.05 Kyle of Lochalsh to Inverness. Strathcarron is a hamlet at the head of Loch Carron, a sea loch where for westbound trains the classic part of the route to Kyle begins, and which can be seen to the right of the picture. Of particular interest was that three of the coaches were in Network SouthEast livery following their transfer to Inverness. Strathcarron is the final passing loop on the line before Kyle is reached. (Eddie Parker)

With the clouds gathering in the hills ahead, 37421 waits at Strathcarron to depart with the 13.12 Inverness Millburn Yard to Kyle of Lochalsh and return infrastructure monitoring train on 16 April 2017. The RETB marker boards and blue indicator lights can be seen ahead of the train, the lights flash when the train is able to proceed.

As this train departs from Strathcarron, a lucky burst of sunlight highlights 37057 on the rear. This locomotive was carefully restored to its original green livery for use in preservation but was sold to Colas in 2015, which retained this livery until recently. On this date, four Class 37s were in Kyle at the same time, two also visiting with the railtour seen in the next picture. Sadly, a badly timed rain shower spoilt the photographic opportunities in the short time they were all together.

On 16 April 2017, 37259 and 37605 pass Attadale with the 09.45 Inverness to Kyle of Lochalsh charter, the 'Spring Highlander' weekend tour run by Pathfinder Tours, which originated at Eastleigh. The tiny station at Attadale can be seen above the second locomotive. A picture like this sums up the attractiveness of the western Highlands in spring!

In 1970, a new road was built between Attadale and Stromeferry alongside the railway to Kyle of Lochalsh to remove the need for the ferry at Stromeferry. Part of this route is vulnerable to rock falls so an avalanche shelter was built to protect the road and railway. From time to time, repairs on this section of line have led to the unique situation where road and rail run on the same formation with appropriate traffic signals. On 2 June 1989, 37415 has just passed through the shelter with the 15.28 Kyle of Lochalsh to Dingwall. (Eddie Parker)

On 28 June 1980, 26024 is seen arriving at Stromeferry with the 10.30 Inverness to Kyle of Lochalsh. At this time, there were sidings here built in the early 1970s to serve an oil rig construction site further down the loch at Kishorn. Although it was only used for a short period, it was instrumental in preventing the closure of the line in 1974. At the time of this visit, the shunter owned by Howard Doris was on site, a Hudswell 0-6-0 named *Tribruit* and numbered D2007. The station building, silo and sidings no longer exist here.

While the Mallaig line quite rightly gets many plaudits, another fine stretch of coastal railway in Britain is the western section of the Kyle line. Originally terminating at Strathcarron, ironically this section was only built for fear of competition from the forthcoming Mallaig extension. 31 rock cuttings had to be hewn out and 29 bridges built and as a result, the cost per mile was £20,000, which at the time was the most expensive railway built in Britain. On 15 March 1989, 37417 *Highland Region* crosses one of the many inlets of the loch near Fernaig with the 10.40 Dingwall to Kyle. (Eddie Parker)

At Craig Farm, near Duncraig, 26018 crosses the causeway with the 11.05 Kyle of Lochalsh to Inverness service on 28 June 1980. Craig is a rare breeds park open to the public. It is interesting to note that of the five coaches in this train, two are non-passenger carrying vehicles for mail, newspapers and parcels.

In another picture taken at Craig Farm, 37428 (named *Loch Long* on one side and *Loch Awe* on the other) passes with the eastbound 'Royal Scotsman' on 3 July 2002. At the time, a couple of the residents were llamas, which can be seen in the picture, one of which would eat anything in sight!

This must be one of the finest locations for railway photography in Great Britain. In bright spring weather with snow on the mountain tops, 37415 is seen on the causeway at Craig Farm with the morning Dingwall to Kyle of Lochalsh train on 16 March 1989. Loch Carron stretches away in the background. Like at other locations, the Class 37 could be heard some 15 minutes before it appeared! (Eddie Parker)

By 14.45 on 28 August 2005, the rain had eased off sufficiently to enable this picture to be taken of 37417 *Richard Trevithick* and 37401 *The Royal Scotsman* passing Craig Farm with Caledonian Heritage Tours' 08.53 Aberdeen to Kyle of Lochalsh railtour. Despite the dull, wet weather, there is still an attractiveness in this wonderful location.

With the Cuillins of Skye in the background, 37416 and 37401 *The Royal Scotsman* pass the attractive Highland Railway station at Plockton with Hertfordshire Railtours' 'Orcadian' landcruise, the 16.18 Kyle of Lochalsh to Inverness, on 26 June 2004. This tour originated at London King's Cross and visited Georgemas Junction next day to let the passengers take a trip to Orkney. At this time, Plockton station building housed an excellent restaurant.

At Drumbuie, the gorse brightens the scene as 37685 *Loch Arkaig* and 37516 *Loch Laidon* pass during a rain shower with the 05.20 North Berwick to Kyle of Lochalsh SRPS special train on 10 May 2014. The village of Duirinish can be seen in the background and its station is just beyond the end of the train. Both villages are in crofting country and Highland Cattle can often be found roaming round Duirinish.

For many years, weight restrictions prevented Class 66 locomotives from using the Kyle line but, when GBRf took over operation of the luxury 'Royal Scotsman' touring train, this problem was soon resolved. The company has two locomotives painted to match the train but, on this occasion, 66736 *Wolverhampton Wanderers* was in charge and is seen at Erbusaig on 13 June 2018 with the 08.39 Kyle of Lochalsh to Boat of Garten.

The magnificence of the scenery near Kyle at Badicaul is clearly in evidence with a background of the Sound of Raasay and the Cuillins of Sky. On 9 July 2008, to complement the scene is 47804 hauling the luxurious 'Royal Scotsman' train shortly after leaving Kyle of Lochalsh at 08.45 bound for Boat of Garten. This is the updated consist of the train as compared to the picture on the title page. In 2012, some of the original coaches (including the saloon photographed at Inverness, though not visible in the title page picture) were retired as it was felt necessary that the train should be able to run at 100mph, although not, it may be added on the Kyle line!

At Kyle of Lochalsh, the railway pier on which the station is situated was created when the railway was built. On 28 June 1980, the whole of the station area is taken up with railway activity as 26024 is released from the buffer stops at about 14.00 after arrival with the 10.30 from Inverness. It can be seen that this busy tourist passenger train includes a buffet car. In the background is the Isle of Skye across the Sound of Sleat. 26024 is preserved at the Bo'ness and Kinneil Railway.

After being released from its train, 26024 spent some time shunting ballast wagons in the sidings on the other side of the station. It is seen here in the cutting leading to the station, where Kyle of Lochalsh signal box is also visible. It is still operational on this date, 28 June 1980, although some rationalisation of the signalling has taken place, leaving the signal gantry bereft of signal arms.

37114 *Dunrobin Castle* is seen shortly after arrival at Kyle of Lochalsh from Inverness on 6 August 1985. Steam heat Class 37/0s were working services on the line at this time, having taken over from the Class 26s, but in a few months, they would be displaced from passenger workings by the newly refurbished Class 37/4s. (Dave Smith)

A herring gull poses for the camera in this view of the terminus station at Kyle of Lochalsh, clearly enjoying the warmth from the locomotive! 37417 *Highland Region* is waiting to depart with the 11.10 to Dingwall on 15 March 1989, during the period after the collapse of the Ness Bridge. Once the departure point for ferries, those to the Outer Hebrides now depart from Ullapool and Uig on Skye. The sidings seen in the earlier picture have been lifted and hard standing is being widened to give road vehicles better access to the shipping berths alongside the pier. (Eddie Parker)

After services were taken over by Class 156 DMUs in 1990, some reallocations took place in the Class 37/4 fleet, meaning that some different locomotives were seen on the 1991 summer trains to Kyle of Lochalsh. 37408 *Loch Rannoch*, formerly a West Highland locomotive, awaits departure with the 17.05 Kyle of Lochalsh to Inverness on 9 July 1991.

With snow on the hills of Skye, 37251 *The Northern Lights* and 37196 await departure at Kyle of Lochalsh on 1 April 1993 with the 08.00 'Cock of the North' InterCity landcruise to King's Cross, as seen earlier at Inverness. This had visited Wick the day before, then travelled to Kyle where passengers were able to get a good night's sleep in the stationary sleeping cars! Five Class 37s were used on the tour: 37196 replaced 37170 at Dingwall on the return from Wick, 37251 and 37196 then being replaced by 37510 and 37078 at Inverness for the run to Edinburgh.

Having heard that the annual visit of the weedkiller to Kyle and the Far North was to take place, the photographer had an overnight journey to Scotland from Yorkshire to photograph it. The reward was this picture at Kyle of Lochalsh, where, in lovely sunshine after a shower, 20904 *Janis* top and tail with 20901 *Nancy* await departure on 31 July 1996. However, as we have seen earlier at Garve, all did not go to plan with this train! (Eddie Parker)

Perhaps because of the story of Bonnie Prince Charlie, there has always been an air of mystique and romanticism about the Isle of Skye. Until the bridge opened, you could even catch a small ferry from Kyle over the sea to Kyleakin on Skye. On the lovely evening of 21 August 1991, 37428 *David Lloyd George* is stabled overnight to form the first train to Inverness the following morning, with one of the Skye ferries also moored overnight on the right of the picture. (Eddie Parker)

Kyle of Lochalsh has always been a popular destination for special trains. One such was on 28 August 2005 when 40145 arrived with Pathfinder Tours' 'Whistling Scotsman', the 10.30 from Aberdeen (and from Birmingham the day before). Class 40s were not common at Kyle in BR days but not unknown either.

Another classic picture at Kyle of Lochalsh as 158715 departs as the 17.13 to Elgin on 12 June 2018. These units have now been the usual trains on this line for over 20 years. In the other platform, the 'Royal Scotsman' had arrived earlier.

Chapter 3

The Far North Line from Dingwall to Wick and Thurso

The Far North Line is an attractive rural railway with scenery that varies from farmland to coast and wild moorland. It is 161 miles by rail from Inverness to Wick on the northeast corner of the Scottish mainland, but only about 100 miles by road. This is because the railway has a very indirect and sinuous route and makes two detours inland north of Dingwall, as shown on the map below. However, the A9 has seen major investment in the Kessock, Cromarty and Dornoch bridges to reduce distance and journey time.

Eventually part of the Highland Railway, the line was built in stages from 1862 to 1874. From Dingwall, the railway runs northeast alongside the Cromarty Firth through Alness to arrive at Invergordon. Continuing to run through farmland, the railway passes Fearn and then Tain before

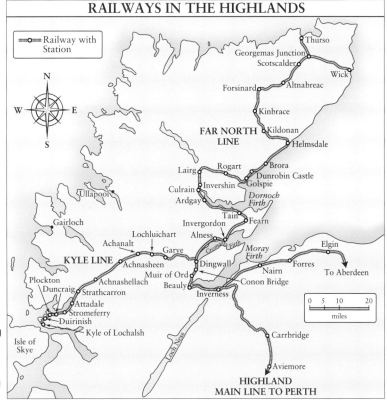

RAILWAYS IN THE HIGHLANDS

This map shows the railways of the north of Scotland and demonstrates well how the Far North Line takes an indirect route to Wick along the banks of the Cromarty Firth and then the Dornoch Firth, before diverting inland at Helmsdale to avoid the difficult route along the coast. The map also shows the Kyle line running to the west coast from Dingwall and the Highland Main Line heading south from Inverness.

taking its first major inland detour, running alongside the Dornoch Firth to Ardgay before climbing to the line's first summit after Lairg (488ft). The line then descends back to the east coast through Rogart to the coastal towns of Golspie, Brora and Helmsdale.

The railway turns inland again here to avoid the high cliffs and deep valleys along the coast, running northwards along the Strath of Kildonan, of gold rush fame. The scenery becomes wilder through the Flow country as Kinbrace and then Forsinard are reached. The line then travels east and the second summit is met at County March (708ft), the remote stations at Altnabreac and Scotscalder are passed before the most northerly junction on the railway system is reached at Georgemas. This is where the branch to Thurso diverges. In past times, trains used to divide here with a portion to serve each destination, now trains reverse to travel to Thurso before returning to Georgemas to travel to Wick.

Motive power is shared with the Kyle line and has changed similarly over the years. Three passenger trains per day ran each way between Inverness and Wick in 1979, today this is four. Additional trains have been introduced south of Lairg as part of the 'Invernet' project to improve access to Inverness for commuting in particular. With the Kyle trains, they combine to give a service of 14 trains per weekday (pre-pandemic) between Dingwall and Inverness. Charter trains also operate occasionally, sometimes including a visit to Kyle.

Freight traffic on the Far North Line has been interesting, with wagonload trains serving the whole line plus others to industries at Invergordon, but these mostly ceased in the 1980s. However, in 1995 a weekly wagonload service started to run again. This became daily when Safeway extended its train in 2000 from Inverness to Georgemas Junction to supply its supermarkets in Caithness and Orkney. Other freight included oil to Lairg, but both of these trains have now ceased.

Trains of pipes for the oil industry and nuclear waste from Dounreay continue to run to Georgemas Junction intermittently. Timber has also been carried by rail in the past and a further trial took place in 2020, which will hopefully lead to further traffic in the future. Class 37s and then Class 66s and surprisingly Class 67s have operated these freight trains.

So the Far North, with its winding rural nature and changing scenery, continues to be attractive to railway enthusiasts, particularly when freight or charter trains operate, and hopefully freight will develop again in the future.

At Dingwall Junction, 67030 passes with the 16.18 Lairg to Inverness discharged oil tanks on Saturday 23 April 2011. These tanks went south to Mossend on the Monday as seen earlier in this book at Slochd Viaduct behind 66434. 67030 would have worked to Lairg light engine from Inverness after arrival with the sleeper service, using time when it would otherwise have been idle. The Cromarty Firth is seen to the right of the locomotive, the Kyle line is in the foreground.

On 1 August 1996, 20901 *Nancy* passes the well-kept station at Invergordon with the Inverness to Wick and Thurso weedkiller. At the rear, Inverness had provided 37401 *Mary Queen of Scots* as a replacement for 20904 *Janis*, which had failed at Kyle the previous day. Invergordon is situated on the Cromarty Firth and, following the oil boom, the former naval base became a place where oil rigs were repaired, serviced or stored. It is now also a stopping off point for cruise ships, enabling their passengers to tour this interesting part of Scotland. (Eddie Parker)

On a hot, hazy day, 47854 *Diamond Jubilee* arrives at Invergordon with the 10.30 Keith to Kyle of Lochalsh 'Royal Scotsman' on 20 July 2013. It then ran round its train, using the passing loop, to return south. It would run round again at Dingwall before proceeding to Kyle of Lochalsh. This is the most northerly picture of a Class 47 in my collection, though one has visited Thurso. 47854 was previously numbered 47604, as seen earlier in this book at Kingussie.

At the rural station of Fearn, 158716 calls as the 06.20 Wick to Inverness via Thurso on 18 June 2011. This design of station is also found at other locations on the southern part of the Far North Line, such as Ardgay. The siding at Fearn has been used for freight traffic in recent times, but it has now been taken out of use.

Heading south from Tain, 37409 *Lord Hinton* is seen bringing up the rear of the 16.32 Dunrobin Castle to Aberdeen 'Northern Belle' on 20 July 2013, 37425 and 37423 are at the front. The train had originated as the 08.43 from Aberdeen. This location illustrates well the farming country that the Far North Line passes through at this point. This luxury train is a rare visitor north of Inverness, but on this occasion the use of three Class 37s meant it was well worth the visit!

On Friday 13 September 1996, 37153 and 37165 are seen shunting at Tain, about to drop off hopper wagons loaded with lime in the sidings at the station. At this time, trains such as this were running to the Far North Line via Aberdeen and Inverness to serve various terminals en route, very much like a traditional freight, picking up and dropping off wagons along the way. The photographer followed the train from Aberdeen and took pictures of it en route, the consist being very different earlier in the day! After Tain, it continued up to Georgemas Junction with the vans and flat wagons. (Eddie Parker)

Staying in Edderton near the railway, I went out after breakfast to photograph the northbound Safeway train, expecting the usual Class 66. Being only a few miles north of Tain on a quiet morning, I heard the distant sound of the train wheels passing slowly through the passing loop there and then the unmistakeable sound of a Class 37 accelerating away! So, I was able to obtain this surprise picture of 37427 with a lightly loaded 02.00 Mossend to Georgemas Junction on Easter Monday 21 April 2003.

Looking north from the bridge over the railway at Edderton, 37411 *The Scottish Railway Preservation Society* and 37418 *East Lancashire Railway* pass by with Pathfinder Tours' 'Orcadian' landcruise, the 13.40 Wick to Inverness at 19.20 on Sunday 20 April 2003. Also in the picture is the closed station at Edderton and the Balblair distillery.

Fifteen minutes earlier, 37411 and 37418 were seen stopped, awaiting time on the causeway over the Dornoch Firth at Easter Fearn with the same train. A better view for the passengers eating their evening meal than the confines of Tain station! This train travelled north on Saturday so the passengers could visit the Orkney Islands overnight.

On 13 March 1989, 37416 heads south from Ardgay with the 12.00 Wick and Thurso to Dingwall. Ardgay is a small village on the south-west shores of the Dornoch Firth. Until 1977, the station was known as Bonar Bridge after the small town about a mile away at the crossing point over the river at the head of the Dornoch Firth. It is one of the busier small stations on the Far North Line with some 7,000 passengers a year. The station has a loop, which is the only one between Tain and Lairg. (Eddie Parker).

At Ardgay on 7 June 2005, 67009 works from Inverness to Lairg light engine to collect the empty oil tanks, which, at this time, returned south on a Tuesday. Owing to their heavy axle weight, Class 67s were limited to a maximum of 20mph between Tain and Lairg. As can be seen from the picture, the station has a very long southbound platform, which can accommodate ten coaches.

With the Kyle of Sutherland in the background, 66107 has just passed Culrain station with a northbound ballast at 20.07 on 6 June 2005. Pictures like this are one benefit of the long summer days in this part of Scotland. A recent landslip had occurred at Helmsdale and the train may have run in connection with this; a similar working took place next day.

Reflected in the waters of the River Oykel, 37415 crosses the gloriously located Invershin Viaduct on 13 March 1989 with a Dingwall to Wick and Thurso service. (Eddie Parker)

In another evening picture at Invershin, this time taken from the north side of the viaduct, 66112 crosses with the 18.43 Inverness to Kinbrace empty timber train at 20.43 on 22 June 2004. This train would be loaded with timber at the lineside after the last passenger train of the day had passed, departing from Kinbrace at 02.55. Despite this innovative approach to reduce costs, the economics were not favourable and the train only ran from 2003 to 2005.

In glorious light, 158728 crosses the viaduct over the River Oykel at Invershin with the 07.21 Inverness to Wick on 6 June 2005. A footway was constructed on the bridge as a millennium project, as seen in the previous picture, meaning that there are now few train passengers travelling the distance of less than half a mile between the stations at Culrain on one side of the bridge and Invershin on the other.

An innovative feature that started in 1999 was the use by Safeway of rail to distribute goods to its supermarkets in Inverness, which was extended to the Far North Line in 2000. As the company did not require a full train north of Inverness, a government grant enabled it to be used by other customers. Here, 66101 approaches Lairg, near Achany, with the 01.40 Mossend to Georgemas Junction at 07.32 on 26 June 2004, with two Safeway containers and five vans of other goods. This service ceased to run in 2005 when Safeway was taken over and supply arrangements changed.

There have been several pictures of the Lairg oil tanks in this book so far, this is the last one! 66103 is seen shunting oil tanks into the terminal on 6 June 2005. At this time, the train ran as the 01.20 (Mondays-only) from Mossend Yard to Lairg, being due to arrive at 14.10 behind a Class 67 but on this occasion, it actually arrived at 16.30.

Under a dramatic sky, preserved D9000 *Royal Scots Grey* arrives in the passing loop at Lairg with the 14.00 Wick to Linlithgow returning 'Far North Explorer' SRPS charter on 18 June 2011. The station, footbridge and waiting shelter are all interesting Highland Railway features. However, this East Coast Main Line express locomotive has not been a regular visitor to the Far North line!

A few minutes later, D9000 departs from Lairg with 37676 *Loch Rannoch* on the rear. The Class 37 had led the train to Thurso and assisted with shunting manoeuvres. The oil terminal can be seen behind the station building. Lairg is a small, dispersed settlement but is a regional centre; Lairg station had an important past role in the delivery of goods, mail, parcels and newspapers as well as being a connecting point for onward bus journeys. A large livestock market also provided rail traffic in past times.

On 17 March 1989, 37419 is seen near Acheilidh with the midday Dingwall to Wick service running downhill after having climbed the 1 in 70 gradient out of Lairg. The railway at this point is making a long detour inland around the Dornoch Firth, whereas the A9 now has a bridge across the mouth of the estuary. There was much local pressure to incorporate the railway into this bridge when it was built but to no avail. (Eddie Parker)

Given the right weather, the north of Scotland is a wonderful place to be in early spring. The superb quality of the air and light combines with stunning views and wildlife along with few visitors and no midges! If Class 37s were the motive power, you could often hear them almost 15 minutes before the train passed you. Such was the case with 37416, which has just passed Acheilidh with the 12.00 Wick to Dingwall service on 17 March 1989. (Eddie Parker)

Further down the bank towards Rogart, the countryside has changed and 37610 *T.S. (Ted) Cassidy 14.5.71-6.4.08* and 37423 *Spirit of the Lakes* run downhill at Ardachu with the 08.20 Inverness to Thurso on 10 October 2010. This train is seen earlier in this book in Glen Carron and is UK Railtours' 'Cock of the North' weekend landcruise from King's Cross.

At Rogart, 66113 is seen leaving the station and passing loop with the 11.28 Georgemas Junction to Mossend freight on 23 June 2004. The signal box can be seen in the left background and is now privately owned, it is the former south signal box and has been relocated nearer to the station.

On 21 September 1996, 37170 passes Rogart station with what was the third freight to Georgemas in a week. Rogart is a request stop set in a beautiful part of northern Scotland, opened in 1868 and closed in 1960 but reopened less than a year later. It is good that such stations stay open as it is used by less than 2,000 people a year, which is also the case for many of the smaller stations on the line. Indeed, most passenger use on the Far North Line is now south of Tain, and government plans indicate that the line may eventually be electrified to Tain from Inverness. (Eddie Parker)

Golspie station is now a private house with listed status. On 27 June 2002, 66114 passes with the 02.00 Mossend Yard to Georgemas Junction with a load of five vans, two Safeway containers and two flat wagons. On some occasions, this service was extended to Thurso as a local building materials supplier received consignments by rail.

Dunrobin Castle was provided with its own private station, now available for public use in summer. Here, 156478 and 156499 call with the 12.05 Wick/12.10 Thurso to Inverness on 7 June 1999. This train ran as two separate portions from Wick and Thurso, combining at Georgemas Junction as locomotive-hauled trains had done. The completion of the Far North Line was aided by the Duke of Sutherland, who built the section from Golspie to Helmsdale. The railway has a short climb either side of Dunrobin as the duke did not want the railway to run between the castle and the shore. Not only did he have his own private station at Dunrobin Castle, he had a private train to use on the line too!

Brora is the next passing loop north from Rogart. 66107 is seen arriving with a lightly loaded 02.00 Mossend Yard to Georgemas Junction freight on 2 July 2002. Brora station is similar to that at Tain and others on the Highland Railway system.

Also at Brora, 26045 arrives with the 11.15 (Sundays-only) Wick to Inverness on 29 June 1980. At this time, only one train each way ran on Sundays, the northbound one bringing the Sunday newspapers! Brora's north signal box can be seen along with the goods yard containing several wagons. There was another signal box at the southern end of the station on the southbound platform.

In a similar view 33 years later, 37425 and 37423 *Spirit of the Lakes* arrive with the 'Northern Belle' luxury touring train on 20 July 2013. Seen earlier in this book south of Tain, this train had run empty from Dunrobin, where its passengers could enjoy the castle, to run round at Brora. 37423 had developed a fault with its speedometer so the locomotives had been shunted to enable 37425 to lead the return journey. 37409 was on the rear.

North of Brora, the railway runs close to the shore as far as Helmsdale; there are some magnificent coastal views to be enjoyed on this part of the railway. At Kintradwell, D9000 *Royal Scots Grey* runs by the shoreline leading the returning SRPS special from Wick on 18 June 2011.

On 3 June 2017, two former Inverness-based locomotives, 37421 and 37025 *Inverness TMD*, approach Portgower at 05.45 with the SRPS 'Far North Explorer' from Edinburgh to Thurso and Wick. This train originated at Edinburgh at 21.49 on 2 June, departed from Wick at 13.40 on 3 June and arrived back in Edinburgh at 00.34 on 4 June, a long day trip! At this point, the railway runs between the pebble beach and the foot of the cliffs. I had intended to photograph this train at Portgower on its return from Wick, but despite sun inland there was a thick mist on the coast.

At the small coastal village of Portgower, 37114 *City of Worcester* and 37419 pass with Hertfordshire Railtours' 'Cock of the North' weekend railtour from King's Cross to Kyle of Lochalsh and Wick, returning as the 16.22 Thurso to Inverness on 6 June 1999. 37114 was a surprise on this train as a pair of Class 37/4s would be expected. When it was based at Inverness in the 1980s, it was named *Dunrobin Castle* and was seen earlier in this book at Kyle and Dingwall.

37416 and 37401 *The Royal Scotsman* are about to leave the coast and turn inland at Helmsdale working Hertfordshire Railtours' 'Orcadian' landcruise, the 06.10 Inverness to Georgemas Junction, on 5 June 2005.

In another picture at Helmsdale, 950001 arrives as the 09.35 test train from Thurso to Inverness on 18 July 2013. North of here, the railway runs up the Strath of Kildonan to Forsinard, the next passing place on the railway. This is about a 30 minute journey, which can cause delays if late running occurs. Helmsdale signal box is disused but nicely maintained.

The Strath of Kildonan is a lovely stretch of country and here 37409 *Lord Hinton* and 37402 *Stephen Middlemore 23.12.1954-8.6.2013* pass Duible with Pathfinder Tours' 'Easter Highlander', the 08.15 Aviemore to Thurso, on 21 April 2019. The viaduct is over the Craggie Water, which joins the River Helmsdale at the left of the picture. The circuitous nature of this railway is emphasised here as it is heading northwest at this point despite its destination being in the north-east!

On 19 October 2008, 37417 *Richard Trevithick* (with nameplate only on one side) and 37401 slowly approach the level crossing and station at Kildonan with UK Railtours' 'Autumn Highlander', the 07.30 from Inverness to Wick. With the River Helmsdale behind the train, this is one of my favourite locations on this line. Kildonan is also famous as being the location of a gold rush in 1869!

Deltic 55022 *Royal Scots Grey* is seen earlier in its journey with the 'Far North Explorer' tour, passing the station and level crossing at Kildonan on 18 June 2011. The crossing is ungated, so trains have to stop and whistle before proceeding, but modernisation is planned. As with the 2017 tour, this one too had set off the previous day and travelled overnight, leaving Linlithgow at 21.54.

Passing Kinbrace is 66101 with the 02.00 Mossend Yard to Georgemas Junction at 11.21 on 28 June 2002. The station is just out of view to the left and the timber loading point just south of that. The softer country round Kildonan has now been replaced with the open moorland of the Flow country, some of the wildest and most remote in Scotland. Here the railway is heading north and climbing from sea level at Helmsdale to the County March summit beyond Forsinard, at gradients of up to 1 in 60.

Also at Kinbrace at 11.42 on the same day, 66108 passes with the empty wagons that had earlier taken pipes for the oil industry to Georgemas Junction and were returning to Hartlepool. Rush hour at Kinbrace! As the pipes are longer than the wagons that carry them, flat spacer wagons are included between each one, which can be seen in this picture.

With almost all of the small settlement of Forsinard in view, 158741 departs as the 12.09 Wick to Inverness on 19 April 2003. Situated in the Flow country, a land of peat bog and lochans, Forsinard is home to a RSPB reserve. The remains of the snow fences are in the foreground.

Now heading directly east, 158713 departs Forsinard with the 10.38 Inverness to Wick on 18 June 2011. The station building has found a new use as the visitor centre for the RSPB reserve. The building itself is similar to that at Kinbrace.

Also at Forsinard, 37409 *Lord Hinton* and 37402 *Stephen Middlemore 23.12.1954-8.6.2013* begin the final stage of the climb to County March summit with Pathfinder Tours' 'Easter Highlander' on 21 April 2019. Also in the picture is 158702 as the 11.56 Wick to Inverness via Thurso; the Class 37s waited outside the station for it to arrive so as not to block the level crossing. The roof of the disused signal box can be seen above the train.

After leaving Forsinard, the next station is lonely Altnabreac, which has no public road access. After that comes Scotscalder, another isolated station, now a well-kept private house. 158730 is seen passing the latter station as the 07.21 Inverness to Wick on 28 June 2002.

Georgemas Junction is the most northerly junction on British Rail. 37416 has just arrived on 31 May 1988 with the six coach 06.35 train from Inverness. Here the train split in two; 37416 took the front portion through to Wick and 37420 (just visible to the right of the disused signal box) backed onto the rear of the train to take its portion through to Thurso. On the return, 37416 would stop with the Wick portion at the island platform while 37420 would run through the station and reverse its portion onto the rear of the Wick coaches. 37420 would then await the arrival of the next northern service. On the left of the picture is the shed where permanent way vehicles were housed. (Eddie Parker)

Georgemas Junction is seen again on 21 September 1996 as 37170 shunts different types of wagons, containing a variety of cargoes, from the Inverness freight. The Friends of the Far North Line are a group that exist to promote the line and its use for passenger and freight traffic. According to them, the weekly Enterprise train carried a variety of traffics, including fridges and freezers, steel plate, agricultural lime, containerised aviation fuel and timber to and from a variety of railheads on the Far North Line. 37170 survives as 97302, in use with Network Rail. (Eddie Parker)

In this view, 37114 *City of Worcester* and 37419 arrive at Georgemas Junction on 6 June 1999 with Hertfordshire Railtours' 'Cock of the North' landcruise, the 08.30 from Inverness to Wick and Thurso. The Thurso branch curves off behind the front locomotive. In the background is the village of Halkirk, the only settlement of any size in this area but whose station closed in 1960 while Scotscalder and Georgemas Junction remained open.

Freight is not plentiful on the Far North Line now, but one of the successes has been the transportation of pipes from Hartlepool to Georgemas Junction. From there, they are taken by road to the Subsea 7 yard at Wick, welded into long pipes then dropped into prepared sea trenches. On 20 September 1996, 37682 *Hartlepool Pipe Mill* and 37517 are at Georgemas Junction as pipes are unloaded. The busiest time for freight on the Far North Line was during the two world wars. In World War One, freight tonnage carried by the line doubled due to transporting military supplies and coal for the fleet at Scapa Flow via Invergordon and coastal shipping. (Eddie Parker)

Purpose-built freight handling facilities were created at Georgemas when the Safeway freight train was extended from Inverness. 66101 has arrived with the 02.00 Mossend Yard to Georgemas Junction on 28 June 2002, run round its train, and reversed into the sidings for unloading of the containers to take place. In the background, a lorry is parked next to rail vans so that they can be unloaded or loaded too.

In the earlier pictures at Georgemas Junction, there were two platforms and a footbridge. In 2012, Direct Rail Services built a small freight terminal with loading gantry, as seen here, to facilitate nuclear traffic from Dounreay to Sellafield. As a result, the island platform and footbridge were removed. In April 2021, a trial run was undertaken to evaluate the suitability of using this crane to offload containers from railway wagons, which hopefully might generate rail traffic in the future. Here, 37421 waits to shunt onto the rear of the SRPS 'Far North Explorer' railtour on 3 June 2017 to take the train to Thurso.

At Sibster, in the flat landscape of Caithness, 37025 *Inverness TMD* leads the SPRS 'Far North Explorer' towards Wick as the 09.47 from Thurso. 37421 is on the rear. Top and tail operation as seen here removed the need for an additional locomotive run round manoeuvre at Thurso. However, at Wick, 37025 ran round to the front of the train to lead it back to Edinburgh. Evidence of 37025's steam heat boiler in operation can be seen in the picture!

The InterCity landcruise pictured earlier at Inverness and Kyle is seen again at Wick after arrival as the 08.15 from Inverness on 31 March 1993. 37251 *The Northern Lights* is reversing out of the station to enable 37170, hiding in the shadows inside the station building, to run round the train. The locomotives had to run round separately as the train was longer than the run round loop.

While Georgemas Junction, Wick and Thurso are frequently seen in photographs, the surrounding area is seen less often. In this rather bleak but compelling landscape, 37401 *Mary Queen of Scots* – deputising for the failed 20904 – passes the River Thurso near Glengolly on the branch to Thurso on 1 August 1996. The train had already been to Wick, so it recessed overnight at Thurso before returning south to Inverness the following day. 20901 was on the rear of the train. (Eddie Parker)

Thurso is the most northerly station in Scotland and has a very similar design to Wick with an overall roof and island platform. 50049 *Defiance* is seen after arrival with the Railway Touring Company's 'Autumn Highlander', the 08.10 from Inverness on 7 October 2007. This preserved locomotive is more often associated with railways such as Paddington to Penzance, so is about as far away from home as possible stood at Thurso! This tour originated at King's Cross and also visited Strathcarron, the line beyond there to Kyle being closed temporarily for engineering work. 55022 *Royal Scots Grey* worked the tour from London to Perth, 40145 and 50049 north of there.

Finally, two pictures of the same train at Thurso. 26044 is seen shunting after arrival with the 11.10 from Inverness, at about 16.00 on 27 August 1979. In these views of a bygone railway age, the station layout is still complete with sidings and a goods shed. Parcels wagons are visible together with a yellow National Carriers parcels van under the trainshed roof, coal wagons for the local coal merchant are in the siding and children are making their way home from school.

26044 has now finished shunting and is ready to depart with the 17.39 Thurso/17.37 Wick to Inverness, which it would work as far as Georgemas Junction. Coal is now being unloaded into sacks on a lorry from the coal wagons, and a sheep market is in progress. All with the cliffs of the island of Hoy in the Orkneys visible in the background!

Bibliography

Dunn, Pip, *From Wick to Penzance: The Story of the Class 37/4s,* Eastfield Media, Spalding (2020)

Fenwick, Keith and Geddes, Howard, *The Highland Railway,* The History Press, Stroud (2009)

Pearson, Michael, *Iron Roads to the Far North and Kyle,* Wayzgoose (2003)

Rhodes, Michael, *Encyclopaedia of 21st Century Signal Boxes,* Platform 5, Sheffield (2019)

Spaven, David, *Highland Survivor, The Story of the Far North Line,* Kessock Books (2016)

Friends of the Far North Line, *FoFNL 25* (2019)

Class 37 Locomotive Group website for checking locomotive and railtour details (www.class37.co.uk)

Class47.co.uk website for checking locomotive details (www.class47.co.uk)

Six Bells Junction website (www.sixbellsjunction.co.uk) for confirmation of railtour details

ScotRail website (www.scot-rail.co.uk) for miscellaneous research